DATE DUE			

Bicycling

Bill Gutman

Capstone Press

M I N N E A P O L I S

Printed in the United States of America.

Capstone Press • 2440 Fernbrook Lane • Minneapolis, MN 55447

Editorial Director   John Coughlan
Managing Editor   John Martin
Production Editor   James Stapleton
Copy Editor   Thomas Streissguth

Library of Congress Cataloging-in-Publication Data
Gutman, Bill.
  Bicycling / Bill Gutman.
    p. cm. (Action sports)
    Includes bibliographical references (p.) and index.
    Summary: Briefly relates the history and development of bicycles before discussing the various styles of bikes and offering safety and maintenance points. Concludes with a glossary of terms.
    ISBN 1-56065-264-0
    1. Cycling--Juvenile literature. [1. Bicycles and bicycling.] I. Title II. Series
    GV1043.5.G88 1996
    796.6--dc20   95-7807
                                             CIP
                                             AC

99 98 97 96 95   6 5 4 3 2 1

Photo Credits: Huffy Bicycles: pp. 8-9, 11; Specialized Bicycle Components: pp. Cover, 4, 12, 22, 24, 41; Trek Bicycle Corporation: pp. 6, 14, 17, 18, 27, 28, 32, 35, 38.

Table of Contents

Chapter 1
The Sport of Bicycling

Bicycling is fun and challenging for young and old, boys and girls, men and women, and entire families. And bicycling is something that can be enjoyed almost all year long.

The bicycle can get you from place to place. It can also be an excellent way to exercise. A good ride on a **touring bike** is a real workout. An off-road ride on a **mountain bike** can be even more challenging.

Biking can be competitive. Many people enjoy BMX racing, while others are now involved with mountain bike racing. There is something for everyone in bicycling. It is fast becoming the family sport of the 1990s.

Chapter 2

A Brief History

There are many stories about the first bicycle. After all, the wheel was invented many thousands of years ago, and a crude way to propel one or two wheels might have been invented soon after that.

Most historians now believe that a Frenchman named Count de Sivrac made the first real bicycle back in 1791. He appeared in a park in Paris on a machine later called a **hobby horse**. It was a wooden frame with wooden wheels attached at both ends.

This first bicycle had no pedals. The rider propelled it by pushing off the ground with his

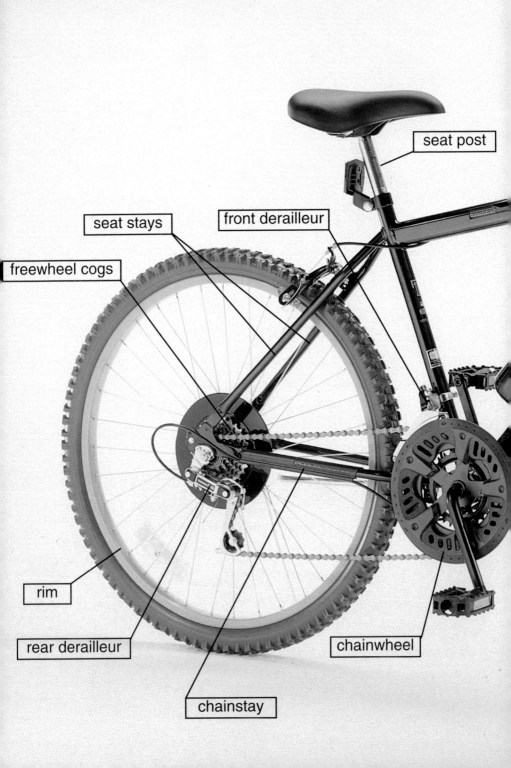

seat post

seat stays

front derailleur

freewheel cogs

rim

rear derailleur

chainwheel

chainstay

handlebar

thumb shifters

top tube

brake levers

cantilever brakes

fork blade

feet, then coasting between pushes. The wheels didn't move, and these hobby horses couldn't be turned, either. To call this a bicycle is really stretching it. But it was a start.

The First Pedals

In 1839, a Scottish blacksmith named Kirkpatrick Macmillan attached a system of levers, which he called treadles, to the rear wheel of a hobby horse. By pushing the treadles up and down, the rider could propel the rear wheel.

As the years passed, these early bicycles slowly improved. Rubber tires first appeared in New York in 1868. Three years later, a bicycle called the "Ariel" was invented by the Englishman James Starley. It had a giant front wheel and a tiny back one.

Nicknamed the **Ordinary**, these bikes became very popular in England and America. They were more comfortable, could travel up to 15 miles (24 kilometers) per hour or more, and could go long distances. In 1884, a young

Special flourescent paint on this BMX bike makes it glow in the dark, for cool night riding.

newspaper reporter named Thomas Stevens rode an Ordinary across the United States in 103 days.

People began to see the kind of fun they could have with bicycles. That was really the beginning of a bicycle boom that has lasted until today.

Modern Bikes

In 1884, John K. Starley, the nephew of James Starley, made the first in a line of bikes called **safety bicycles**. The safety bikes had two new mechanical inventions. They were the first bikes made with a chain-and-sprocket, rear-wheel drive. This made the safety bike easier to steer and easier to drive forward.

By the 1890s there were millions of bicycles being produced each year. A company in Chicago was selling the bikes for as little as $7 to $12. That made them even more popular.

The bicycle boom in North America slowed in the early part of the 20th century, when automobiles were becoming popular. By that time, the bicycle looked much like it would look for the next 50 years. It had thick rubber tires, a metal frame, and just one gear.

Bikes would remain popular over the years, but a new kind of bike would not appear until the early 1960s. After that, a new age of the bicycle would begin, and new and better bikes would be introduced regularly.

Chapter 3
Bicycles Today

There are several different styles of bicycles that are popular today, including the touring bike, the **BMX bike**, and the mountain bike. These bikes are better than ever, with frames that are stronger and lighter. Some bikes even have shock absorbers, much like cars. The various gears make them easier to ride.

Heavyweights and English Racers

The **heavyweight** wasn't much different from the safety bicycles that were popular early in the century. This bike had strong steel frames and level handlebars. It also had wide seats and wheels that were 24 or 26 inches across.

The heavyweight also had wide balloon tires with steel fenders to protect the rider from mud and water. The bike had just one gear and used **coaster** brakes controlled by the pedals. This was a strong and durable bicycle that could really take a beating. But it was also heavy. With a single speed, it wasn't good for long rides.

The **English racer**, also called a middleweight bike, appeared in the 1960s. Like the heavyweights, these bikes had wide seats, straight handlebars, and metal fenders. Most middleweights also had 24- or 26-inch (60- or 65-centimeter) tires that were narrower than heavyweight tires. At first, English racers had three gear speeds.

The middleweights were light, all-purpose bikes. They had brakes on both the front and rear wheels, with the brake levers on the handlebars. Later, they carried ten gear speeds.

Touring bikes are best for long-distance travel.

They were much better than the heavyweights for long trips because of their weight and their range of gears.

The Touring Bike

The modern touring bike grew out of the English racer. Originally called ten-speeds because of their gears, these are lightweight bikes that have small, hard seats and thin, hard tires.

On these bikes, the handlebars are curved downward, making the grips much lower. The rider bends forward as he pedals. The bikes don't have fenders of any kind. Their **caliper** brakes work on both wheels. The brake levers are on the handlebars.

These are very useful bikes and probably the best kind for long-distance riding. Today they are made out of special lightweight materials. Some of them weigh as little as 20 pounds (9 kilograms). Instead of having ten speeds, many bikes today have 18 or more gears to choose from. That gives riders a gear for any riding condition.

Touring bikes are now available in a wide variety of sizes. The cheaper models cost as little as $100. Top models can cost several thousand dollars. There are a wide variety of accessories (such as a luggage rack) available for special uses.

Mountain bikes can handle off-road trails, steep slopes, obstacles, and all kinds of weather.

Special models of touring bike are used for racing on a track or road. They are also used for the bicycle stage of the triathlon, a very popular sport. The touring bicycle is probably the most popular bike being sold today.

The BMX Bike

In some ways, the small BMX bicycle is a smaller version of the old heavyweight bike. The BMX bike has thick, 20-inch tires and a strong frame. Most models weigh between 20 and 30 pounds (9 and 13.6 kilograms). There is also a smaller version with 16-inch tires for very young riders.

These bikes have a single gear, like the old heavyweights. But unlike the heavyweights, they have caliper brakes on both the front and rear tires. The rider controls the brakes with levers on the handlebars.

The street version of the bike, also called the small wheeler, has a large seat and sometimes a rear fender as well. It may come with coaster brakes. The bike was designed for general riding by youngsters. So the BMX has to be rugged to stand up to the beating it will take.

BMX stands for bicycle motocross. BMX bikes are used for all kinds of trick riding and jumping. In addition, BMX racing has become a popular sport. There are special accessories for trick bikes, while racing BMX bikes have no fenders and just a single back brake.

The Mountain Bike

Mountain bikes are the latest in bicycles. They began to appear in the 1970s, but it wasn't until the 1980s that mountain biking became really popular.

Believe it or not, the idea for the mountain bike came from the smaller BMX bike. Adults in California watched young people ride off-road with their BMX bikes. The adults wanted to try it, but the thin-wheeled touring bikes they used were just not rugged enough to take that kind of pounding. The result was the invention of the mountain bike.

The handlebars of mountain bikes are set out straight, giving the biker more stability on rough trails.

Mountain bikes have very durable, lightweight frames. They have thick, rugged tires and strong wheels. Their handlebars are straight. For quick stops, the bike has powerful hand brakes on both the front and rear wheels.

Unlike the BMX bikes, mountain bikes have many gears for climbing hills and for other kinds of riding. Mountain bikes can also be very expensive. Basic models cost as little as $100 to $150. But the best bikes with a full range of new features can cost $3,000 or more.

Today's Mountain Bikes

The frames of modern mountain bikes are longer than those of touring bikes. There is more space between the frame and wheels. This allows the bike to move easily through mud and other rough terrain. The forks of the better mountain bikes also have a built-in **front suspension** system. This works almost like the shocks on a car. The forks give a smoother ride with less stress on the rest of the bike's frame.

Good mountain bikes have 15 **gears** or more and have three chainwheels and six back sprockets. Mountain bikes also have a **cantilever** brake system, which is needed for the fat, rugged tires. It's the best brake system ever put on a bicycle. The bikes come in a variety of sizes, so you can pick the one that is best for you.

Chapter 4
Bicycle Safety

No matter what kind of bicycle you ride
and no matter what type of riding you do, there
are certain rules of safety you should follow.
Bicycle riders should know these rules. They
should also know how to take care of their
bikes. If you love riding, you also love your
bike. You'll want to care for it as well as you
can.

Wear the Right Clothing

The single most important piece of gear for
any bicyclist is the helmet. It's now a law in
many states that riders must wear a helmet

when riding a bike of any kind. No matter where you live, you should wear a helmet, whether you are out for a slow ride around the block or if you're climbing a rough trail on a mountain bike. There are no exceptions to this commonsense rule.

There are different types of helmets for different types of riding. Open-face helmets just cover the head. They are good enough for touring riders or for those out for an easy Sunday ride. Full-face helmets cover the top and the sides of the head and much of the face, including the mouth. BMX and mountain bike racers should always wear this type of helmet. If not, they can wear a separate visor or mouthguard.

Racers should always wear long-sleeve shirts and long pants. They can get special padded clothing or add their own knee pads and elbow pads. Gloves protect the hands and give riders a better grip.

Those riding on long tours or bike hikes in warm weather may be tempted to wear shorts

Open-face helmets cover the top and sides of the head. This allows the biker a clear sight of the road.

and tank tops. You should wear elbow pads and knee pads, too. Remember—everyone falls or slips at some time. If you don't have protection, you can be injured.

Get Your Skill Level Up

Make sure that your riding skill matches the type of riding you want to do. If you are going to ride on the roads, make sure you are a confident rider. Pay attention to traffic

conditions, and never weave from side to side or out into the line of traffic.

Always stay to the right and ride with the traffic. Observe all the traffic laws. You must stop at red lights and at stop signs. Know the hand signals for right turns, for left turns, and for slowing down. Never ride on a sidewalk where pedestrians are walking.

With a bike that has 10 speeds or more, make sure you can shift gears quickly and confidently. You shouldn't have to fumble around if you need a low gear to climb a hill quickly. Using the wrong gear can cause you to swerve into the flow of traffic.

If you want to do tricks on your BMX bike, start slowly. If you take a big jump at full speed without having done it before, you could really wipe out. Go over small jumps first, then work your way up to the bigger ones.

If you decide to ride off road and climb hills on a mountain bike, start slowly. You need to be in good shape to peddle up a rough hillside. While riding downhill or on narrow trails, you may come upon obstacles, like thick brush, branches, or rocks. Know how to get around these before you go into really rough country.

Learn How to Race

There are many racing events for BMX and mountain bikes. BMX racing is very similar to motocross racing with motorcycles. Mountain bikers race against the clock and against other riders on rugged downhill **obstacle courses**. There are also uphill-downhill and cross-country mountain bike races.

All of these require great skill. In BMX racing you must know how to go over jumps, take both banked and flat turns, and handle bumps called whoop-de-doos. Learn what the courses are like. Try to practice with your friends. If you go up against six or seven riders without practicing, it could be a rough road.

Mountain bikers can do amazing things on their bikes–but the riders have to be good, too.

Riding off-road is one thing. You can learn at your own pace, both by trial and error and by watching others do it. But once you're racing, you're going at top speed. Prepare by learning just what your bike can and can't do. Figure out how it will react to bumps and jumps, rocks and branches. Work with the brake system, so you know how much pressure to apply to both the front and the rear brakes.

Any time you race, there's a chance of a wipe out. Learn how to take a fall to avoid injuring yourself. Always check yourself and your bike after a wipe-out, even a minor one. Don't race against bikers whose skill level is a lot higher than your own.

Follow these rules and you'll have a better chance to enjoy safe biking, even at top speeds and over the roughest terrain.

Chapter 5
Bicycle Maintenance

You don't have to be an expert mechanic to take good care of your bike. But you should know the basics of bike maintenance. A sound bicycle will serve you better than one that is in need of repair or new parts. If you know the signs of wear, you can find a problem before it comes up during a long trip or in the middle of a tough race.

A Few Check Points

If you use your bike regularly, you should make it a habit to check it out both before and after you use it. This is especially true if you take a long trip, if you use the bike for very rough riding, or if you race.

You also should learn some basic maintenance and repair. For example, you should be able to change a tire, repair a tube, adjust your brakes, replace the brake pads, adjust the seat and handlebars, and tighten any bolts that get loose.

Here is a basic list of things to check on your bicycle. If you can cover these basics, chances are your bike will always be in top shape. Going through this checklist will help you spot serious problems. If you find something you can't repair yourself, get it checked out and repaired by a pro.

1. Carefully check all the weld joints on the frame for any signs of cracking. Rough riding can cause even the best frames to crack at some time.

2. Check your brake pad alignment. Make sure the bottom of the pad is even with the edge

Small packs that fit on the frame or handlebars make touring bicycles handy for long-distance riding.

of the rim's braking surface. If not, adjust it. If a small ridge has formed on the pad, carefully cut it away with a razor blade.

3. Always check and tighten any loose bolts on your brake levers, your shifter levers, the stem, handlebar, and bar ends.

4. Check the weld area of the stem for cracks. With a standard stem, periodically remove it, then clean and grease the quill.

5. Make sure the ends of your brake and shifter cables are not frayed or blocked. Also, check the outer casings for cracks or kinks.

6. Examine your tires for worn and torn **knobbies**. Look for any cuts and tears.

7. Make sure the valve stem stands out straight from the tire. If it's standing at an angle, you have let some air out of the tire. Hold the spokes and pull the tire. The stem should slide back into place.

8. Check and tighten any loose bolts on your drivetrain. This includes the chainwheel bolts, crank bolts, pedal spindles, derailleur fixing bolts, and the rear derailleur pulley wheel bolts.

9. Take a close look at the ends of the derailleur cables to make sure they are not frayed.

10. Look for signs of cracks where the stem clamps to the handlebar. Loosen the handlebar and slide it to the side. You can then see if the clamps are hiding any cracks.

Each Type of Bike is Different

All of the above rules don't apply to every bike. Some small-wheelers still have coaster brakes. BMX bikes don't have derailleurs and gears. Touring bikes don't have knobbies on the tires. Know your bike and the various parts. Try to find a repair manual for your bike. The more you know about it, the better off you'll be.

Doing a small, inexpensive repair now can save you a big, costly one later. And if the time comes to buy a new bike, follow this one basic rule: always buy the best bike you can afford.

Chapter 6
The Long Tour

Many people love to plan their holidays and vacations around biking. Vacation bicycle tours are offered in many parts of the United States and Canada. Riders love to just take off for a day on their own and ride their bicycles for hours. They might stop for lunch or even spend a night at a motel. It's a great way to improve your physical health while enjoying the sights and sounds of the countryside.

There are a few things that should be kept in mind on a long trip. Plan the trip carefully. Know where you are going and how you will get there. You might take a side trip or two, but keep to your main plan. This is especially important if you are planning to stay somewhere overnight. You will want to get there before dark.

Watch the weather. If stormy or bad weather is predicted, don't go. Dress appropriately. If the weather cools down in the late afternoon, bring along extra clothing. If the sun is bright and hot, some sunscreen will help. Your helmet will keep the sun off your head.

Packing too much will weigh you down and slow your trip. Take only what is absolutely necessary. Lightweight touring bikes and all other kinds of bikes can be fitted with luggage racks and other means to carry gear.

Tools and Supplies

Prepare for the worst: one of your party can't continue because a bike has broken down. That can make it difficult for everyone. If you are going to be far from home, make sure someone in the group has the proper tools for minor repairs. These include screwdrivers,

Headlamps and lightweight battery packs are available for most types of new bikes.

pliers, wrenches, a tube repair kit, and an extra tire or two. A member of your group can carry extra brake pads, a chain or two, and any other spare parts you might need. And don't forget an air pump.

It's important to bring other supplies, including a first-aid kit, plus enough fluids to replace what you lose through perspiration. Most bikes have a place for a water bottle, even two. Make sure everyone has water or a fluid-replacement drink such as Gatorade. Extra fluids might also be a good idea. You can replace them when you reach a general store or a service station.

You might also want to bring along some food. Make sure it's something that won't spoil in the heat. If you are going to be peddling for hours, you will work up an appetite. Remember to bring some money, in case you need to buy supplies or use a telephone. And make sure your friends and family know where you will be.

Bicycling is a great sport. With touring bikes, BMX bikes, and mountain bikes, it offers something for everyone. Safe and healthy biking should be the goal for everyone. Once you choose the kind of biking you want to do, then learn all you can about it. Learn about your bike, what makes it work, and take good care of it. Then go out and enjoy.

Glossary

BMX bike–small, tough bicycles used mostly by kids for freestyle riding and BMX racing. These bikes have 20-inch tires. Their name stands for bicycle motocross.

caliper brakes–the brake system on touring and some BMX bikes in which brake pads squeeze both sides of the wheels to stop the bike.

cantilever brakes–a powerful braking system used on many mountain bikes, operated by hand levers on each side of the handlebars

coaster brakes–brakes that are applied by stepping backwards on the pedals. Coaster brakes lock the rear wheel only.

English racer–the first series of lightweight bikes with thin tires and three different gears.

The English racers began the bicycle revolution in the 1960s.

front suspension–a system of shock absorbers built into the front forks of the bicycle. Many high-tech mountain bikes use this type of suspension.

gears–the chain-to-sprocket ratios that change the force needed to turn the pedals. The lower gears are for climbing, and the higher gears are for cruising and racing.

heavyweight–bicycles made from about 1900 to the early 1960s. They had heavy frames, thick tires, metal fenders,and just a single speed.

hobby horse–the nickname for the very first type of crude wooden bicycles, which appeared in France about 1800

knobbies–the knob-like projections on BMX and mountain bike tires

mountain bike–a very popular bicycle that has a rugged but lightweight frame, thick tires, and straight handlebars. Mountain bikes are used for a variety of off-road riding and climbing, as well as racing.

obstacle course–a bicycle course with many natural obstacles such as bumps, holes, brush, branches, and rocks. Mountain bikers enjoy riding and racing over off-road obstacle courses.

Ordinary–a popular early bicycle that had a huge wheel in front and a small wheel in the back. The Ordinary first appeared in the early 1870s.

safety bicycle–an early bicycle that introduced the chain-and-sprocket rear-wheel drive. These were the first bikes to give the rider mechanical help in propelling the machine forward.

touring bike–the thin-wheeled, multi-geared bikes that are used for road riding, long tours, and road racing.

To Learn More

Lafferty, Peter and David Jefferis. *Pedal Power: The History of Bicycles.* New York: F. Watts, 1990.

Murphy, Jim. *Two Hundred Years of Bicycles.* New York: Lippincott, 1983.

Stine, Megan. *Wheels! The Kids' Bike Book.* Little, Brown, 1990.

Wilhelm, Tim. *Bicycling Basics.* New York: Prentice-Hall, 1982.

Some Useful Addresses

American Bicycle Association
P.O. Box 718
Chandler, AZ 85244

U.S. Cycling Federation
1750 E. Bouler Street
Colorado Springs, CO 80909

Canadian Cycling Association/Association cycliste canadienne
1600 James Naismith Drive, Suite 810
Gloucester ON K1B 5N4

Bicycle Museum of America
435 E. Illinois Avenue
Chicago, IL 60611

Bicycling Magazine
33 E. Minor Street
Emmaus, PA 18098

Index